T0006681

EPIC
ADVENTURES

WRITTEN BY
SAM SEDGMAN

ILLUSTRATED BY
SAM BREWSTER

FOR MY PARENTS, WHO TAUGHT ME TO TRAVEL – SAM SEDGMAN

KINGFISHER
LONDON & NEW YORK

Text copyright © Sam Sedgman 2022
Illustration copyright © Macmillan Publishers International Ltd 2022
First published 2022 in the United States by Kingfisher,
120 Broadway, New York, NY 10271
Kingfisher is an imprint of
Macmillan Children's Books, London
All rights reserved

Distributed in the U.S. and Canada by Macmillan,
120 Broadway, New York, NY 10271

Library of Congress Cataloging-in-Publication Data has been applied for.

ISBN 978-0-7534-7801-1

Kingfisher books are available for special promotions and premiums.
For details contact: Special Markets Department, Macmillan,
120 Broadway, New York, NY 10271

For more information, please visit
www.kingfisherbooks.com

Printed in China
1 3 5 7 9 8 6 4 2
1TR/1121/UG/WKT/128MA

Senior designer: Jeni Child
Senior editor: Elizabeth Yeates

EU representative: 1st Floor, The Liffey Trust Centre,
117-126 Sheriff Street Upper, Dublin 1 D01 YC43

EPIC ADVENTURES

WRITTEN BY
SAM SEDGMAN

ILLUSTRATED BY
SAM BREWSTER

KINGFISHER
LONDON & NEW YORK

ALL ABOARD!

There is no finer way to travel than by train. For 200 years, trains have clanked, rumbled, and whooshed across our planet, letting passengers from bustling cities and tiny villages gaze out of the window and watch the world go by.

And what a world it is. Trains cut through thick forests where grizzly bears swipe salmon from rushing streams. They shake cherry blossoms from trees beside ancient temples. They heave gold from within deep mines in scorching deserts. They plunge into tunnels beneath mountains and soar on bridges above the sea. They take us to school, to work, to see family and friends. They bring us adventure. And they bring us home.

Every train journey has a story to tell. Why was it built? Where does it go? Who travels on it, and why?

This book will help you discover those stories for yourself, by taking you on 12 of the world's most incredible railroad journeys. See how ordinary people live and travel in different countries. Witness how railroads have shaped nations—through war and battle; trade and business. Discover incredible feats of engineering that is now seared into the landscape by human hands.

Some of these journeys are modern and lightning-fast, shooting between cities in a matter of hours.

Train journeys are as varied as the world.

Others clatter through endless fields, forests, or deserts for thousands of miles, taking many days and nights to reach their destination. Some are elegant and luxurious; some are raucous and crowded. Some are from the present; some are from the past. All of them, in their own way, are extraordinary.

So you won't just find facts about trains in this book. These adventures are also about the people, places, food, animals, customs, and cultures you might discover as you explore the world by train.

Although some of the trains you'll see are from history, almost all of the journeys in this book can be taken by train today, and every line, track, and station is real.

For each of the 12 journeys, you'll see a map of the railroad showing the amazing places the train travels through, and a close-up from the route to bring the journey to life. There are also special feature spreads following

each journey. There's plenty of unexpected and fascinating things to see—so keep your eyes peeled.

The world is waiting for you! Get ready for adventure, and climb aboard.

Sam Sedgman

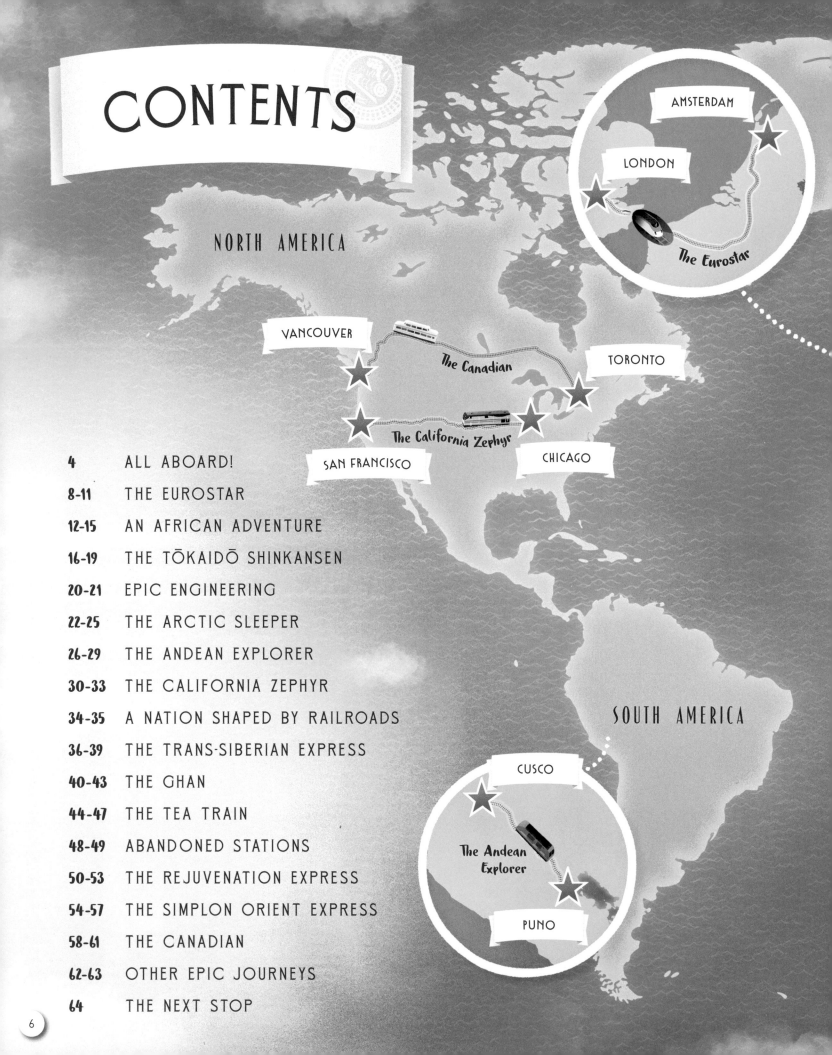

CONTENTS

AMSTERDAM

LONDON

The Eurostar

NORTH AMERICA

VANCOUVER

The Canadian

TORONTO

The California Zephyr

SAN FRANCISCO

CHICAGO

SOUTH AMERICA

CUSCO

The Andean Explorer

PUNO

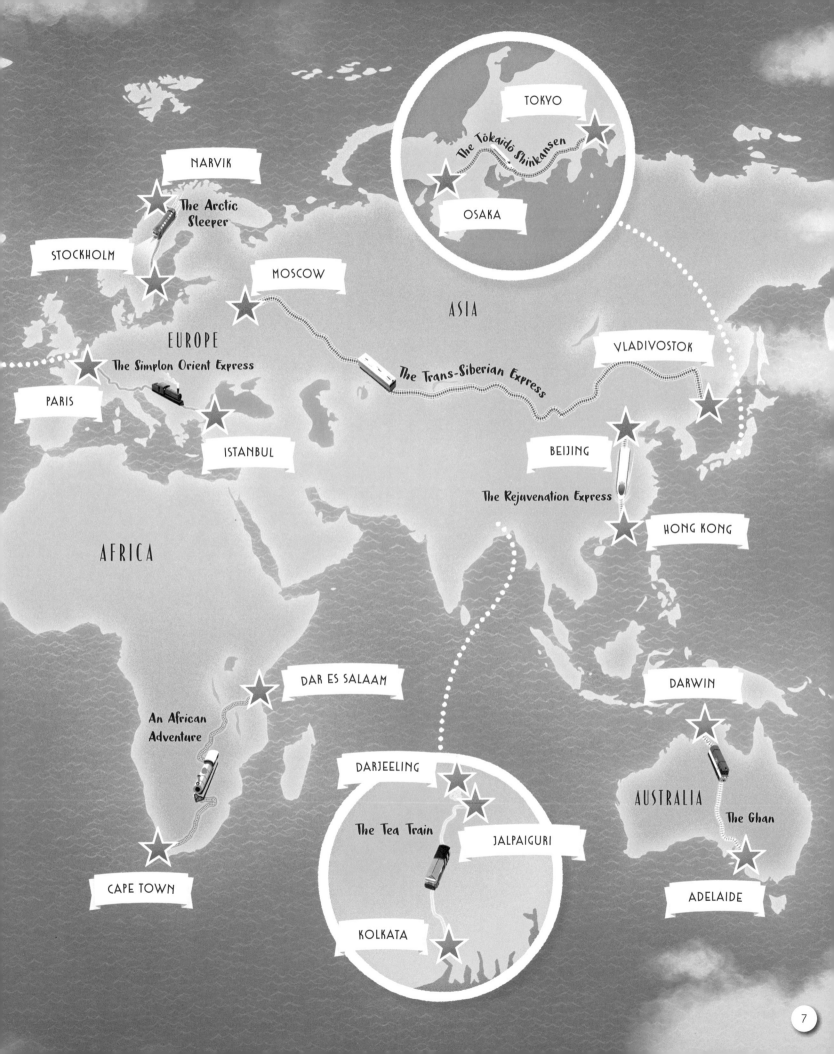

NARVIK

The Arctic Sleeper

STOCKHOLM

MOSCOW

TOKYO

The Tōkaidō Shinkansen

OSAKA

ASIA

EUROPE

The Simplon Orient Express

VLADIVOSTOK

The Trans-Siberian Express

PARIS

ISTANBUL

BEIJING

The Rejuvenation Express

HONG KONG

AFRICA

DAR ES SALAAM

DARWIN

An African Adventure

DARJEELING

AUSTRALIA

The Ghan

The Tea Train

JALPAIGURI

CAPE TOWN

KOLKATA

ADELAIDE

THE EUROSTAR
LONDON TO AMSTERDAM

LONDON

Founded by Romans 2,000 years ago, London grew into a wealthy global superpower and was the heart of the British Empire. Once the world's most populous city, London built the first ever underground railroad to cope with overcrowding. Today, it is one of the most diverse cities in the world.

LONDON

The Thames barrier protects London from floods caused by tidal surges.

The White Cliffs of Dover are made of chalk. A recognizable landmark when crossing by ferry, the cliffs are an important symbol of Britain.

DOVER

The Channel Tunnel is the longest undersea tunnel in the world.

Samphire Hoe nature reserve was reclaimed from the sea. It was built using more than two million tons of earth dug up to create the Channel Tunnel.

The English Channel is the busiest shipping area in the world.

In 1910, French railroad stations banned kissing on their platforms because trains were being delayed by too many romantic goodbyes.

The UK is connected to the rest of Europe by the Channel Tunnel—an engineering masterpiece under the raging sea. The Eurostar line from London to Amsterdam travels through the tunnel, linking the hearts of two former empires in a matter of hours. The train ride is also a cleaner, more comfortable alternative to the busiest air route in Europe.

Rotterdam is the largest port in Europe.

AMSTERDAM

NETHERLANDS

Land reclaimed from the sea is known as a polder. The Dutch reclaimed land by building dikes and draining the seawater inside using pumps powered by windmills.

ROTTERDAM

Meaning "low-lying land," half of the Netherlands is three feet above sea level. Since the land is so flat, biking is very popular. In fact, there are more bicycles than people. The country's famous windmills once ground crops into flour, but today power the country's trains. Every Dutch train runs on wind power!

AMSTERDAM

The capital city of the Netherlands, Amsterdam is built on swampland and held up by eleven million long poles sunk into the earth. It has more canals than Venice, crisscrossed by more than 1,200 bridges. During the Dutch Golden Age of the 17th century, Amsterdam was the wealthiest city in the world.

DELTA WORKS

Hundreds of burial sites in Belgium honor the soldiers of many nations who died in World War I.

BELGIUM

One of the seven wonders of the modern world, a complex system of enormous dams and sluice gates called the Delta Works protect the Netherlands from flooding.

ANTWERP

Antwerp is world famous for its diamonds.

Known as the flower shop of the world, 80 percent of the world's flower bulbs are grown in the Netherlands.

BRUSSELS

Brussels is the political center of Europe.

Belgians invented roller-skates and the saxophone, and may even have invented French fries—which they eat with mayonnaise.

LILLE

FRANCE

EUROSTAR STATS:
Distance: 221 miles
Time: 3 hours 52 mins
Top speed: 186 mph

9

THE CHANNEL TUNNEL

Modern tunnels are built by tunnel boring machines (TBMs). They are long, snake-like contraptions that cut through 10 metres of earth a day with rotating teeth at their front. Conveyer belts shift the rock away through the tunnel, and as the machine digs farther, rings are placed into the freshly dug walls to reinforce them.

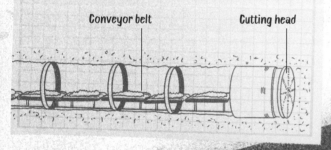

Conveyor belt   Cutting head

BRIGITTE

The French named their TBMs Brigitte, Catherine, Europa, Pascaline, Severine, and Virginie. When the tunnel was complete, they were dismantled and put in museums. The British machines had no names, but two were made to burrow into the earth after the tunnel was built, and they're still there today!

Workers in the tunnel navigated through the earth using gyrotheodolites—machines that use a spinning device called a gyroscope to find north.

Many large fossils, some 93 million years old, were found beneath the sea bed when digging the tunnel.

AVIGNON

PARIS

The Eurostar links London to cities in France, Belgium, and the Netherlands—and from there, trains to almost all of Europe.

Five hundred trains pass through the tunnels every day, including passenger trains, freight trains, and shuttles carrying cars.

Trains can be more than 1,300 feet long. Engineers use bicycles to get from one end to the other when inspecting them in their depots.

The trains move so fast, the drivers can't see the signals by the track. They flash up on screens inside the cabin instead.

Digging under the Channel began in 1987 and the tunnel opened in 1994. At the time, it was the largest and most expensive engineering project ever undertaken. There are three tunnels— two railroad tunnels and a smaller service tunnel between them.

The French and English dug their tunnels at the same time. When they met, the two teams shook hands. They didn't quite meet in the middle though—the English team dug a greater distance.

Dec 1st 1990

The flame lily is the national flower of Zimbabwe.

DAR ES SALAAM

A THIRST FOR STEAM

It's hard to find water in the desert, so many African steam engines used special "condensing" boilers that recycled used steam back into their water tank. Fueling their furnaces with many tonnes of coal, these giant Class 25 locomotives could haul passengers and goods up to 500 miles without stopping.

The coconut crab is the largest crab in the world.

MOZAMBIQUE

MALAWI

TANZANIA

The slow growing mpingo tree is known as the music tree. Its wood is used to make woodwind instruments.

Fruit sellers greet passengers at stations, selling avocados, bananas, rice, and sweets.

KAPIRI MPOSHI

TAZARA LINE

Lake Kariba is one of the largest human-made lakes in the world. The flooded underwater valley is full of drowned trees.

ZIMBABWE

CHISIMBA FALLS

LAKE KARIBA

TAZARA LINE

The railroad from Dar Es Salaam to Kapiri Mposhi was built by China in the 1970s to help landlocked Zambia export its copper to Asia. Copper is a valuable metal, used mainly to make wires and pipes.

BULAWAYO

LIMPOPO RIVER

Termite hills in Zambia can grow up to 33 feet high!

ZAMBIA

LUSAKA

VICTORIA FALLS

HWANGE NATIONAL PARK

BOTSWANA

KALAHARI DESERT

Around 2,000 languages are spoken in Africa, around one-third of the world's total. Dar Es Salaam's name comes from the Arabic word meaning "house of peace." Victoria Falls is also named Mosi-oa-Tunya, which is Lozi for "the smoke that thunders."

The spectacular Victoria Falls was named for Queen Victoria by Scottish explorer David Livingstone. The railroad bridge was deliberately built close enough to the waterfall for travelers to feel the spray.

AN AFRICAN
ADVENTURE STATS:
Distance: 3,604 miles
Time: 15 days
Number of countries
crossed: 5

AN AFRICAN ADVENTURE

DAR ES SALAAM TO CAPE TOWN

Foreign empires fought over southern Africa for centuries, with devastating consequences for the people who lived here. Railroads strengthened these empires' control, extracting valuable resources, such as copper and gold. Today, the influence of former British, Dutch, Portuguese, and German empires remain, as do their railroads. Rumbling from the white sands of the Swahili coast, they pass through the heart of modern Africa, linking thriving, fast-growing cities, frothing waterfalls, and scorching savannas rich with wildlife.

Johannesburg is home to City Deep, South Africa's largest dry port—an enormous rail yard, where freight trains bring cargo from the sea.

The city of Kimberley grew around an enormous diamond mine now called "Big Hole."

South Africa has hospital trains called "Phelophepas" with doctors, dentists, and opticians on board, traveling to rural towns. The name "Phelophepa" means "good, clean health."

PHELOPHEPA TRAIN

Crunchy mopane worms are eaten as a delicacy in Botswana.

Two thirds of flower species in the Cape Town region can't be found anywhere else on Earth.

GABORONE

TSHWANE

ESWATINI

JOHANNESBURG

LESOTHO

THE BIG HOLE

KIMBERLEY

SOUTH AFRICA

ORANGE RIVER

KAROO NATIONAL PARK

GQEBERHA

CAPE TOWN

CAPE TOWN

Known as South Africa's "mother city," Cape Town was founded by the Dutch as a stopping point on long sea voyages to their colonies in Asia. When it was later controlled by the British Empire, many steam engines that powered African railroads were built in Scotland and brought to Cape Town on ships. Some sank and are still at the bottom of the sea.

AN AFRICAN SAFARI

Cheetahs can run up to 70 mph—faster than any other animal in the world.

Giraffes' tongues are so long that they can clean their ears with them. Their tongues are dark, which may protect them from sunburn.

Springboks are the national animal of South Africa. They can jump more then six feet straight up in the air. It's called "pronking."

Africa's largest snake is the African rock python. It can eat animals up to the size of an antelope.

Lions sleep up to 20 hours a day.

Chameleons can change color to adjust their body temperature.

Rhinos wallow in mud to keep cool and prevent insects from biting them. An African white rhino can weigh more than 5.5 tons.

BOTSWANA

Mostly covered by the Kalahari Desert, Botswana is believed to be the birthplace of the modern human species about 200,000 years ago. Cave paintings and other rock art have been discovered there that date back 100,000 years.

The Black Mamba is one of the world's deadliest snakes. It's fast, aggressive, and its venom is highly toxic.

The must see "Big Five" animals when on an African safari are the lion, leopard, rhinoceros, elephant, and African buffalo. Once considered the hardest animals to hunt by foot, the term is still used today by tourists hoping to spot them in the wild.

"Safari" is the Swahili word for "journey."

The flightless ostrich is the largest bird on Earth, and lays the world's biggest eggs.

An elephant can sniff out water from miles away using its trunk. Their long and sensitive nose has up to 40,000 muscles and is both strong enough to tear down trees and delicate enough to pick up tiny twigs. An elephant will use its trunk as a snorkel when swimming!

The aggressive hippopotamus is one of the deadliest mammals in the world, killing hundreds of people a year. With its eyes, ears, and nostrils on the top of its head, a hippo can see, hear, and breathe while the rest of its body is underwater.

Buffalo are believed to hold grudges and have been known to attack people who harmed them years later.

BIG GAME HUNTING

Illegal hunting—called poaching—puts many animals' survival at risk. Rhinos and elephants are killed for their horns and tusks. Elephant tusks are made of ivory, which was once used to make piano keys and jewelry. Rhino horns are ground into a powder, which some people believe acts as medicine. In reality, rhino horns are made of keratin, the same material that makes up your fingernails.

Leopards are solitary animals. They warn other leopards to stay away by making claw marks on trees and marking their territory with their pee and poop.

15

Eating raw fish (sashimi) is common in Japan. The country is surrounded by rivers and oceans, so fish is a major food source. Eating meat in Japan was rare until 100 years ago.

In the shadow of Mount Fuji sits the test track for the fastest train in the world. Hovering above the track using magnets, the prototype L0 Series Maglev train has a top speed of 375 mph. Maglev means magnetic levitation.

Rebuilt after fires, lightning strikes, and sieges by samurais, Osaka Castle is more than 500 years old and one of Japan's most famous attractions.

As Japan's cultural center, Kyoto is famous for its ornate shrines and temples. It was Japan's capital for 11 centuries and today is home to big tech companies, such as Nintendo.

KYOTO

NAGOYA

OSAKA

A highway off-ramp runs right through an Osaka office block.

TOYOHASHI

Tōkaidō Road was a trail from Kyoto to Edo (modern day Tokyo). The 319-mile journey was usually made on foot. Travelers could stop at the 53 resting places for sleep and food. Today, it is the busiest transport route in Japan.

OSAKA

Called "the nation's kitchen," Osaka is famous for its food. Delicacies include takoyaki (fried balls of octopus) and okonomiyaki (a savory pancake often made with cabbage, meat, and seafood). A crucial port, Osaka was the hub of Japan's economy for centuries and today is a big financial center.

Tokyo survives huge rainstorms by draining floodwater into man-made underground caverns the size of soccer stadiums.

TOKYO

Home to 38 million people, futuristic Tokyo is the largest megacity in the world. A small fishing village 5,000 years ago, today it has grown into a sprawling metropolis famous for neon skyscrapers and edgy fashion.

TOKYO

Two-thirds of Japan is covered with forests.

SHIN YOKOHAMA

MOUNT FUJI

SHIN FUJI

THE TŌKAIDŌ SHINKANSEN

TOKYO TO OSAKA

In 1964, the first high-speed railroad opened in Japan and changed rail travel forever. The Shinkansen is lightning fast, spotless, and on time to the second. Whizzing from Tokyo to Osaka along the Tōkaidō line, the journey follows an ancient path walked by travelers for centuries. The line has grown into one of the busiest rail systems in the world, and is a symbol of modern Japan: a thriving society forged from ancient culture and tradition.

TŌKAIDŌ SHINKENSEN STATS:
<u>Distance</u>: 320 miles
<u>Time</u>: 2 hours 22 mins
<u>Top speed</u>: 177 mph

THE TŌKAIDŌ

The bullet shape makes the Shinkansen faster and reduces the loud "boom" noise when it rushes into tunnels.

Running on their own special track, the Shinkansen don't have to slow down for other trains. The lines avoid sharp bends by tunneling through mountains, and the earthquake-proof tracks sit wide apart. The first Shinkansen ran at 137 mph—twice as fast as other trains.

乗り場 10:39 →11:27   乗り場   12:1
り場   番 12:14 →13:56   り場   番 11:2
番乗り場 11:27 →14:07   番乗り場   10:3

Vending machines are everywhere in Japan and sell almost everything—eggs, soup, shirts, umbrellas, diapers, and even cars!

EXIT 出口 ↑

In Japan, it's rude to eat or drink while walking or standing, and while riding on most trains. Eating on long-distance trains like the Shinkansen is okay, as long as you avoid eating something smelly, dropping crumbs, or making noise while you eat.

Japanese railroads are famously punctual. If a train is more than five minutes late, passengers are given a "delay certificate" to prove it to their boss or teacher.

SHINKANSEN

The world's five busiest stations are all in Japan.

In Japan, it's polite to slurp noodles while you eat them!

Japanese stations play musical jingles when trains arrive and depart. Each station's jingle is unique and helps passengers recognize the station by sound.

OMIYAGE

Omiyage are edible souvenirs designed to be given to friends, family, or classmates after a trip. A big social taboo if you don't bring something back with you, so there's often a cart selling omiyage on the Shinkansen, in case you forget.

EKIBEN

Ekiben are special boxed meals sold at train stations in Japan. Many are unique to each station, showcasing local dishes. People travel Japan's railroads just to sample the different meals. Regions take great pride in their ekiben. Some come in boxes shaped like trains or animals, and some even play music while you eat.

駅弁

THE FORTH BRIDGE

This symbol of Scotland crosses the Firth and Forth, a large estuary where several rivers meet. Three pairs of cantilevers, or large beams, balance the structure as it stretches outward. These are anchored to pillars in the water. Until 2011, a team of painters worked constantly to maintain its red color.

EPIC ENGINEERING

THE ELBLĄG CANAL

Boats on the Elbląg Canal in Poland become amphibious trains, ascending and descending by rail between steep sections of the waterway.

THE GOTTHARD BASE TUNNEL

The Gotthard Base Tunnel in the Alps is the longest railroad tunnel in the world. At 35 miles long, the portals are so far apart that the weather can be completely different at either end.

THE TAUSHUBETSU BRIDGE

Nicknamed the "phantom bridge," the Taushubetsu Bridge is a railroad bridge in Japan that is no longer used. Every May, it becomes submerged by water when a nearby dam adjusts the river flow. The bridge starts to reappear in January.

GRAND CENTRAL TERMINAL

Grand Central Terminal in New York City has 44 platforms—more than any station in the world. Its size is matched by its elegance—it's famous for its oyster bar and a gold mural of the zodiac on the ceiling.

The world's railroads are made up of bizarre and beautiful structures, and jaw-dropping feats of engineering. Here are some of the most impressive and interesting constructions around the world.

THE QINGZANG RAILWAY

The Qingzang Railway reaches 16,000 feet above sea level—the highest point of any railroad in the world. The high-speed trains that run on this railroad are pulled by special diesel engines built to burn fuel at high altitude, where there is half as much oxygen in the air as normal. A doctor travels on board to help passengers with altitude sickness.

THE TRAIN TO THE CLOUDS

Rising from the Chilean coast to the city of Salta in Argentina, The Train to the Clouds crosses the awesome La Polvorilla Viaduct at 13,845 feet above sea level.

THE ØRESUND LINE

The Øresund Line links Copenhagen, Denmark with the Swedish city of Malmö. A 5-mile bridge carries the railway and a road from mainland Sweden to a manmade island in the sea, before diving into a tunnel and emerging 2.5 miles later near the Copenhagen airport. The tunnel was built so planes could avoid the bridge when landing.

THE ARCTIC SLEEPER

— STOCKHOLM TO NARVIK —

Travel to the *Arctic Circle* by sleeper train from bustling Stockholm in Sweden to the remote Arctic town of Narvik in Norway. As the train heads north, the air gets colder, and sprawling forests give way to glassy lakes and looming mountains.

Tjuonavagge lies just outside Abisko National Park. This huge U-shaped valley is the gateway to Sápmi, the northern region of Scandinavia.

Narvik was once a fishing village, but its thriving port now ships iron ore and other cargo all over the world.

ABISKO

KIRUNA

NARVIK

Fjords are steep valleys carved by melting glaciers. They are a familiar sight in Scandinavia.

When the land around the mining town of Kiruna became unstable, the town was moved to a new home 5 miles away. Some buildings were dismantled and rebuilt, while others were moved by trucks in one piece. The slow move gave the town the nickname the "millipede town."

Whales and dolphins are a common sight off the Norwegian coast.

The Swedish word "flygskam" means "flight shame"—an embarrassment to fly because it's bad for the environment. Cheap and efficient trains are one way Sweden's travelers go green: trains emit far lesss pollution than planes.

ARCTIC SLEEPER STATS:
Distance: 872 miles
Time: 19 hours
Number of stops: 18

There are 30,000 islands around Stockholm. A group of islands like this is called an archipelago.

Trains in Sweden drive on the left, but cars drive on the right.

Ten percent of the world's wood comes from Sweden, where more trees are always planted than are cut down. Over half of the country is covered in forest.

Passengers can eat warm bowls of reindeer stew, as the train rattles into the Arctic Circle where the specular Northern Lights appear and the barriers between day and night melt away.

Traditional wooden cottages in Sweden are painted "falu red." This hardy paint was invented by recycling the waste from the Falun copper mine.

STOCKHOLM

Built over fourteen islands, Stockholm is one of the cleanest cities in the world – they recycle 99% of their household waste. Sweden is so good at recycling, they import rubbish from other countries to recycle it for them!

Rockets and balloons are launched from nearby Esrange, Europe's largest civilian space center. The empty Arctic wilderness makes it a perfect launch site.

The ice hotel in Jukkasjärvi, Sweden is made entirely of ice. Guests sleep on reindeer hides and in polar sleeping bags on a beds made from ice. The hotel melts each summer and is rebuilt for winter.

The indigenous Sámi people live in Sápmi, the northern parts of Norway, Sweden, Finland, and Russia. They are skilled fishers and shepherds, but are best known for reindeer herding.

Beautiful colors appear in the night sky above the Arctic Circle. Aurora borealis, or the Northern Lights, are caused by collisions of tiny particles in the atmosphere, creating waves of color and light.

THE ARCTIC CIRCLE

The Arctic Circle is an imaginary line that runs about the top of Earth. Here, in the middle of summer, the Sun never sets—so there's sunshine throughout the day and night. In the middle of winter, the Sun doesn't rise at all, so it's always dark.

REINDEER

Reindeer thrive in the cold North. The Sámi use reindeer to pull sleds, use their fur and hides to make clothes, and their bones and antlers to make tools. Reindeer have four stomachs (like cows), which may help their body clocks to work, so they know when to sleep during the confusing light summers and dark winters.

24

Reindeer are so important to Sámi, many attend classes to learn how to care for their animals!

Before the railroad, ore was moved by reindeer sleds.

The Sámi divide the year into eight seasons instead of four.

THE OFOTEN LINE

This 27-mile stretch of track cuts through steep snowy mountains to carry ore from iron mines to the Narvik port. Snaking past cascading waterfalls, these freight trains can haul more than 8,800 tons, among the heaviest in Europe.

267

Bromeliad

THE STATS:
Distance: 455 miles
Time: one day and one night
Highest point: 14,000 feet

MACHU PICCHU

The abandoned mountaintop city of Machu Picchu was built by the Incas almost 600 years ago. Made without cement, its carved stone walls survived centuries of earthquakes. Each stone was carried up the mountain by hand.

OLLANTAYTAMBO

CUSCO

The trains carry oxygen to help passengers fight "soroche"—high altitude sickness caused by the thin mountain air.

At 14,396 feet above sea level, the La Raya Pass is the highest point on the journey.

Many modern fabric-weaving techniques were invented in Peru before 500BC

ANDES MOUNTAINS

The Andean Condor is the world's largest flying bird. It has a wingspan of 10 feet.

LA RAYA

THE
ANDEAN EXPLORER
CUSCO TO PUNO

The line uses five switchbacks to climb the steep mountain. Locals call it "El Zig-Zag."

From a city once considered the center of the world, this train rumbles from Incan ruins in cloud-capped rain forests, through windswept mountain grasslands and bustling Peruvian markets, as it travels southeast toward one of the highest lakes in the world.

PERU

Colorful woolen ponchos have been worn in Peru since before the Incas. Spanish settlers tried to end local weaving in favor of European textiles, but the traditional techniques survived. Today, Peruvian ponchos are very fashionable.

Llamas and alpacas are related to camels. Llamas are larger and work the land like horses.

Alpacas are smaller, bred for their soft wool, which is warmer than sheep's.

High altitude and moisture in the Andes create "cloud forests" bursting with life.

CUSCO

Once the capital of the Incan Empire, Cusco ruled much of South America until the Spanish invaded in the 1500s. Today, thriving markets and busy plazas sit among cathedrals and temples, with Peruvian street parties a common sight.

More than 5,000 colorful varieties of potatoes are grown in Peru. The invading Spanish introduced potatoes to the rest of the world.

Rail buses with wooden seats run along the railroad, for Peruvian locals only.

BOLIVIA

AYAVIRI

Almost 12,500 feet above sea level, Lake Titicaca is South America's largest lake. The Uru people live on floating islands in the lake, built from layers of totora weed. Their houses are made from it too.

The world's most expensive coffee is made from beans eaten by wild Peruvian civets. The beans are picked out of their poop!

JULIACA

TITICACA

The Incas ruled the Andean mountains from the 12th to the 16th century, building great cities and ornate gold temples. Having no wheels, or writing system, their empire used a network of relay runners, called "chaskis," who moved supplies and information across the land.

PUNO

The capital of Peru's folklore, the city of Puno is known for its songs and dances, such as the "diablada"—the dance of the devils.

LA PAZ

Cable cars carry passengers through the sky in La Paz—a hilly and crowded city in Bolivia.

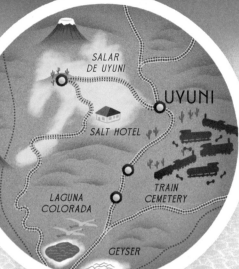

In southwest Bolivia lies the world's largest salt plain—the Salar de Uyuni. The ground here is flat and made of salt that stretches thousands of miles. The 64 million tons of salt were left behind when prehistoric lakes dried up.

When it rains, the plain becomes the planet's largest mirror.

Most of the locomotives in the cemetery were built in the U.K. Some of them have never been used.

THE RAILROAD GRAVEYARD

Uyuni is the nearest town to the salt plains. There were once plans to build a big network of railroads from the town, linking it to nearby cities and ports, but the plans fell apart. The engines brought here to drive the routes were abandoned, and left to rust in a train cemetery.

Since salt makes metal rust faster, the abandoned engines have corroded much quicker than they would have if they'd been kept undercover.

UYUNI

Because it's big and flat with clear skies, scientists use special instruments brought to the salt plain to check the height of satellites in space.

The trains that do run through Uyuni are cargo trains, moving important chemicals and metals, such as copper.

There are more than 100 abandoned steam trains in the graveyard. Most have been stripped for parts.

Salt hotels have been built on the plains. The walls, floor, tables, and chairs are all made from salt bricks cut from the ground. In the rainy season, some parts dissolve and need to be rebuilt

South of the Salar is the salt lake of Laguna Colorada. Minerals and algae have turned the water a dark red color; folklore claims it is the blood of the gods.

The CALIFORNIA ZEPHYR

Chicago ☞ San Francisco

This rail journey, thundering through vast plains, thick forests, snowy mountains, and scorching deserts, is one of the most breathtaking in the world. It charts the path of the first transcontinental railroad and the 19th Century settlers who surged across the continent toward the Wild West, seizing land from Native Americans and plundering mountains for gold. This line tells the story of America, old and new.

A great cheer went up as the line's last rails were secured by a golden spike in 1869. Instead of months, travel from New York to San Francisco now took only a matter of days.

In 1848, the discovery of gold in the California foothills led to a flood of new settlers hoping to strike it big.

The 1,450-mile-long Colorado River runs from the Rocky Mountains all the way to Mexico, via the Grand Canyon in Nevada.

Towering at 272 feet, a sequoia known as General Sherman is the largest tree in the world.

RENO — THE BIGGEST LITTLE CITY

NEVADA

SALT LAKE CITY

UTAH

OAKLAND

LAKE TAHOE

HOLLYWOOD

SAN FRANCISCO

CALIFORNIA

SIERRA NEVADA

COLORADO RIVER

SAN FRANCISCO

After traveling across seven states, passengers disembark in Emeryville in the city of Oakland, which is located across the glittering bay from San Francisco's Golden Gate Bridge. Here, cable cars take visitors the up steep hills and the island prison of Alcatraz glowers in the bay. Head south and you'll find Silicon Valley, birthplace of the microchip and home to technology giants.

CALIFORNIA ZEPHYR STATS:
Distance: 2,438 miles
Time: 51 hours 20 minutes
States crossed: 7
Stops: 34
Tunnels: 43

MISSOURI RIVER

ROCKY MOUNTAINS

WYOMING

MOFFAT TUNNEL

FRASER.
WINTER PARK

DENVER

COLORADO

NEBRASKA

OMAHA

The first transcontinental railroad started in in Iowa in 1863. Seen by many as a sign of progress, it helped settlers seize land, but devastated many indigenous communities.

CHICAGO

IOWA

MISSISSIPPI RIVER

The enormous Mississippi River drains water from 31 of America's 50 states.

ILLINOIS

More than 92 million acres of corn is grown each year in the USA. That's almost the same amount of land that makes up the country of Norway.

CHICAGO

One of the world's most scenic train journeys begins in Chicago, the USA's largest rail hub, famous for the first steel skyscraper, deep dish, pizza, and its basketball team, the Bulls. Chicago was once the fastest growing city in the world, and a vital staging post for many pioneers journeying West in search of employment, land, and gold.

In the 19th Century, settlers flocked to Omaha as a major stopping point on their way farther west in search of new lives. Settlers made their journey on paddle steamers on the Missouri River, then by train through the Rockies. Omaha flourished as a staging post and transport hub, and was nicknamed "The Gateway to the West."

Boy scouts helped patrol stations and level crossings to help the Zephyr's "dawn-to-dusk" dash.

CROSSING

PIONEER ZEPHYR

The gleaming silver Pioneer Zephyr was the first train to run part of the transcontinental railroad at speed. In 1934, it traveled from Chicago to Denver in a record "dawn to dusk" dash of 13 hours. The Zephyr's curves and long lines were part of a design movement called Streamline Moderne, which captured America's imagination. Soon, Zephyr-mania swept the country. Cars and airplanes were renamed "zephyr" to cash in on the phenomenon.

The first passengers on the Pioneer Zephyr included a mascot— a small donkey named Zeph!

In the style of the Zephyr, even things that didn't move much were made to look streamlined, such as buildings, vacuum cleaners, and toasters.

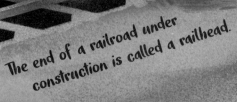

The end of a railroad under construction is called a railhead.

CALIFORNIA ZEPHYR

The train that runs the Chicago to California route today is called the California Zephyr. Mainland America is so big it's divided into 4 time zones—Eastern, Central, Mountain, and Pacific time—and on this journey passengers will reset their watch twice. It takes only 4.5 hours to fly from Chicago to San Francisco, but each year more than 400,000 people travel the 51 hours on the California Zephyr. With windows on every side, observation carriages allow passengers to take in the sights as they make their way across the country.

Zephyr means "a wind to the West."

CHICAGO

The line was built in pieces by different companies. They were paid by the mile, so they raced against each other to lay the most distance. Cutting through rough terrain was made possible by using dynamite, and the two companies raced to blow up the same mountain.

From snowy mountains to scorching deserts, the line copes with all types of weather and terrain. In Nevada, the hot sun can warp the rails; During Chicago winters, frozen rails are set on fire to melt any ice. In the Sierra Nevada mountains, snow sheds help to prevent trains from being buried by avalanches.

LONDON

The world's first underground railroad opened in London in 1863. They were powered by steam, which filled the tunnels with smoke and soot. Today, the trains are electric.

THE FIRST RAILROAD

Before railroads, wagons were pulled over crude tracks of wood or stone. The world's first journey on iron rails was at Merthyr Tydfil in Wales, where iron ore and 70 passengers were hauled 9 miles by a steam locomotive.

RAILROAD DECLINE

Affordable cars and fast highways made trains less popular starting in the 1950s.

THE NIGHT MAIL

Trains made communication faster—mobile post offices shifted mail around the country, sorting it en route. Letters and packages were picked up and dropped off without the train stopping, using carefully placed nets and catapults.

STEPHENSON'S ROCKET

Passengers and freight have been traveling by steam train since the Stockton and Darlington line opened in 1825. Five years later, Stephenson's Rocket was the first steam engine to connect two cities—Liverpool and Manchester.

THE NEED FOR SPEED

Rival companies battled it out to have the fastest and most comfortable long-distance trains. Their elegant, aerodynamic engines became symbols for the Golden Age of steam travel. In 1938, a locomotive called Mallard set the world speed record for a steam train by reaching speeds of 126 mph.

HIGH-SPEED TRAINS

Trains became popular again in the 1970s when new diesel-powered express trains linked cities at 125 mph.

TUNNEL BORING MACHINES

Today, more people travel by train in the UK than ever before. TBMs dig long tunnels quickly, allowing new train lines to be built more easily.

A NATION SHAPED BY
RAILROADS

The birthplace of the steam engine, Britain's engineers unleashed the Industrial Revolution on the world.

In 19th Century Britain, iron rails began snaking through fields and forests, delivering coal to fuel the furnaces of thousands of factories. Trains delivered food, mail, and other deliveries to cities and towns. They let people and ideas criss-cross the country, reshaping the nation forever. Today, trains remain embedded in the landscape: an emblem of the past, and a promise of the future.

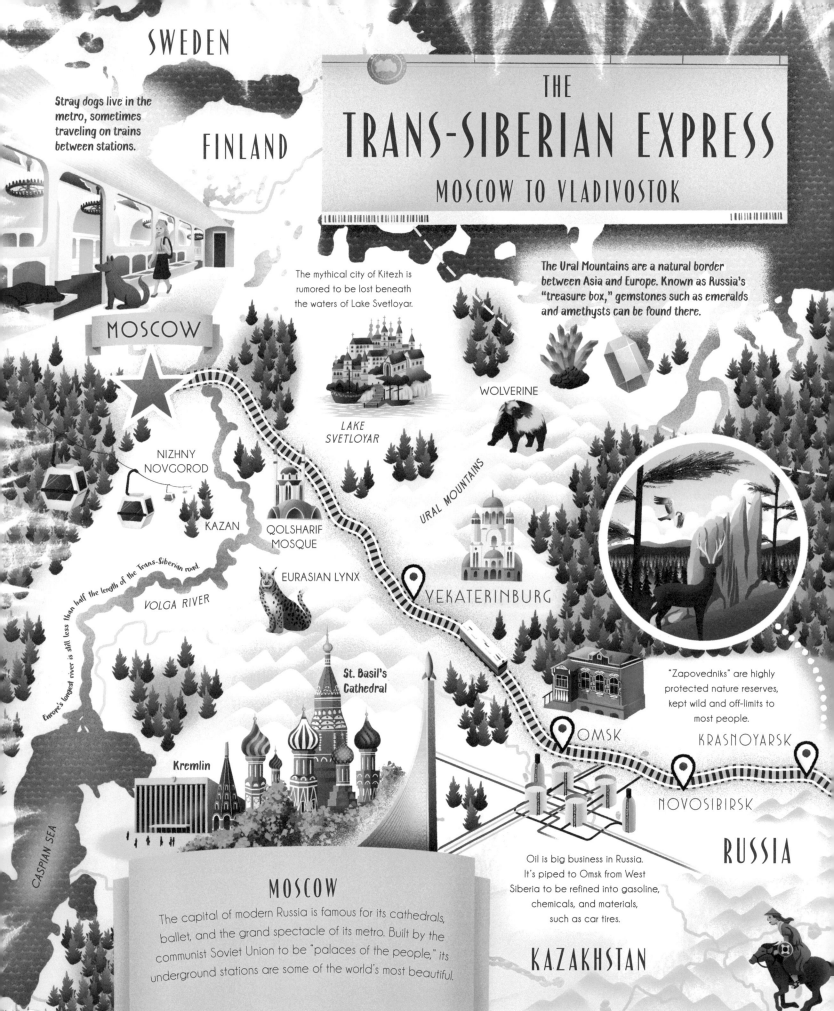

SWEDEN

FINLAND

Stray dogs live in the metro, sometimes traveling on trains between stations.

MOSCOW

The mythical city of Kitezh is rumored to be lost beneath the waters of Lake Svetloyar.

The Ural Mountains are a natural border between Asia and Europe. Known as Russia's "treasure box," gemstones such as emeralds and amethysts can be found there.

LAKE SVETLOYAR

WOLVERINE

NIZHNY NOVGOROD

KAZAN

QOLSHARIF MOSQUE

URAL MOUNTAINS

YEKATERINBURG

EURASIAN LYNX

Europe's longest river is still less than half the length of the Trans-Siberian road.

VOLGA RIVER

St. Basil's Cathedral

Kremlin

"Zapovedniks" are highly protected nature reserves, kept wild and off-limits to most people.

OMSK

KRASNOYARSK

NOVOSIBIRSK

RUSSIA

CASPIAN SEA

MOSCOW

The capital of modern Russia is famous for its cathedrals, ballet, and the grand spectacle of its metro. Built by the communist Soviet Union to be "palaces of the people," its underground stations are some of the world's most beautiful.

Oil is big business in Russia. It's piped to Omsk from West Siberia to be refined into gasoline, chemicals, and materials, such as car tires.

KAZAKHSTAN

The longest rail journey in the world links Moscow to the Sea of Japan. Forged under Tsar Nicholas II, the railroad has survived two revolutions, a civil war, and the rise and fall of the Soviet Union. Today, the steel spine of Russia travels through mountains, forests, and the Siberian wilderness, carrying the heavy loads of the country's factories and farms, along with chattering families visiting friends.

ARCTIC CIRCLE

EURASIAN BROWN BEAR

KAMCHATKA PENINSULA

SEA OF OKHOTSK

Called "The Pearl of Russia," Lake Baikal is the world's deepest lake. Before tracks could be built around it, trains crossed on rails laid onto its frozen surface. It's said a carriage full of gold stolen from the last Tsar in the revolution derailed, tumbling into the lake, where it remains to this day.

VLADIVOSTOK

A thriving port city at the eastern edge of Russia, Vladivostok is where the Western and Eastern worlds meet. It was closed to foreigners until 1991, but today the city is a gateway to Asia—you can take a ferry to Japan

TRANS SIBERIAN EXPRESS STATS:
Distance: 5,772 miles
Time: seven days
Number of cities crossed: 30

Kamchatka crab

FIN WHALE

Salted BBQ fish

IVOLGINSKY DATSAN BUDDHIST TEMPLE

The average January temperature at the line's coldest part is -28°C.

SKOVORODINO

KHABAROVSK

LAKE BAIKAL

ULAN-UDE

IRKUTSK

The railroad track in Mongolia is wider than in Russia. Trains are lifted up to have their wheels changed.

CHINA

SEA OF JAPAN

TRAIN TO BEIJING

Ulan-Ude is the finish line of the Mongol rally, a yearly 10,000 mile car race from Europe.

MONGOLIA

VLADIVOSTOK

FERRY TO JAPAN

THE RAILROAD OF REVOLUTIONS

The Trans-Siberian Railroad was the dream of Tsar Nicholas II, who wanted to unite distant Siberia with the rest of Russia. But when a revolution in 1917 forced him to step down, the railroad became a major tool in the battle for Russia's future.

In the Russian civil war, over 300 armored trains were used by the Red Army to support battles.

The civil war between the Bolsheviks, or the Red Army, and the anti-Bolshevik White Army lasted for three years, with the Reds victorious.

The symbol of communism is the hammer and sickle—the tools of the factory worker and farmer.

The Trans-Siberian Railroad was one of the main highways of the war.

After seizing power in 1917, Vladimir Lenin and the Bolsheviks wanted to make Russia a communist country. Communism imagines a society where everyone is equal and wealth is shared. But the Bolsheviks faced huge opposition, and civil war broke out.

In 1918, the Tsar Nicholas II and his family were taken by train to Yekaterinburg, where they were executed. This ended years of rule by monarchy.

Fabergé eggs are beautiful ornaments decorated with precious gems. An egg commemorating the Trans-Siberian Railroad was made for Tsar Nicholas II, with a small train of gold and platinum hidden inside.

Food and work were scarce in Russia in 1917, so workers rioted, forcing the rich tsars from power. When little changed, another revolution led Lenin and the Bolsheviks to power.

Supplies to build the railroad were brought from all over the world, with ships navigating through freezing rivers.

Some war trains printed newspapers on board, sharing their side's political propaganda across Russia.

Telegraphs were used to send and receive orders from war trains.

Powerful artillery shells could turn the tide of battles.

DECAPODS

Trains were pulled by enormous steam engines called decapods. One was so big it straightened the curves of track and had to be retired.

Russian criminals were exiled to Siberia, often sentenced to hard labor, including building the railroad line.

Millions of extinct woolly mammoths have been preserved beneath Siberian permafrost since the last ice age. Today, they are dug up for the ivory from their tusks.

THE GHAN

ADELAIDE TO DARWIN

Traveling through the vast, remote, and scorching "Red Center" of the Australian Outback, riding the Ghan is a journey unlike any other. The European settlers who built the railroad northward from South Australia first arrived there in the early 19th Century, seizing land from Indigenous peoples who had lived in the country for tens of thousands of years. This railroad tells the story of Australia old and new—its extraordinary people, climate, animals, and history.

The Outback has one of the clearest night skies in the world. Here, huge telescopes gather data on stars and galaxies. In the Southern Hemisphere, Australia's stars are completely different from the stars you see at night in the Northern Hemisphere.

The Flying Doctor Service travels to medical emergencies in remote places.

ULURU

At the heart of the Red Center stands Uluru—a single enormous sandstone rock, half a billion years old. It's a holy site to the Aboriginal people who live nearby, with many ancient stories about its origins. It's said if you take a piece of Uluru away, you will be cursed. Some tourists who took small rocks as souvenirs tried to mail them back after experiencing bad luck.

The Indigenous peoples of Australia are the world's oldest surviving civilizations, living in Australia for more than, living on the continent for more than 50,000 years. Since ancient times they have shared their lore and history through wood carvings and by painting icons and symbols on rocks. Rock art found in Western Australia is estimated to be around 40,000 years old.

ALICE SPRINGS

At Australia's heart, Alice Springs was built along the Todd River, which is completely dry for most of the year. The river was named for Sir Charles Todd, who built the telegraph line linking Adelaide to Darwin. The railroad follows its path. The town was named for Todd's wife, Alice.

THE GHAN STATS:
Distance: 1,851 miles
Time: 3 days
Average speed: 53 mph
First journey: 1929

DARWIN

The railroad brings goods from the south to Darwin's port, which links the country to Asia and the rest of the world. Darwin's port was so crucial to Australia during the Second World War that Japanese aircraft bombed the city to destruction.

KATHERINE

NITMULUK GORGE

Freshwater crocodiles ("freshies") are native to Australia and live in its lakes and rivers. They usually aren't dangerous to humans and will flee quickly. This is unlike the larger saltwater crocodiles ("salties") that live near the sea, and often ambush their prey, sometimes swallowing it whole.

HOTEL

ALICE SPRINGS

TODD RIVER

Australia is wider than the Moon.

Australia's ecosystem is unique and carefully protected. It's the only place you'll find wild marsupials, such as kangaroos, koalas, and wombats.

MARLA

LAKE EYRE

LAKE TORRENS

LAKE FROME

It would take 27 years to see every Australian beach if you visited one each day.

ADELAIDE

KANGAROO ISLAND

ADELAIDE

Adelaide was built by British settlers in 1836, who named it after King William IV's wife. Before they arrived, the indigenous Kaurna people called the area Tarndanyangga, which means "land of the red kangaroo." European settlers renamed many Australian places. Today, many jurisdictions have a dual naming policy, where both traditional and colonial names are used.

It took 120 years to build a railroad from Adelaide to Darwin. The first line from Adelaide was begun in 1878, arriving in Alice Springs 50 years later. The Ghan hauled crucial cargo along the route for nearly 100 years. But sandy soil and flooding made the track unstable, and in 1980 a new route was opened. The final section to Darwin was only completed in 2004.

Before roads and the railroad were built, camels would carry goods and people through the desert. The camels traveled in lines, known as trains.

Australia has more wild camels than anywhere in the world.

Camels were brought to Australia in the 1800s to help navigate the Outback, which was too hot for horses. Camel drivers from Turkey, Egypt, and Afghanistan helped build the railway.

AUSTRALIA'S RED CENTER

AUSTRALIA'S POOP PROBLEM

European settlers brought cattle to Australia in 1788 to be farmed on ranches. But the dung beetles that normally cleaned up the poop in Europe didn't exist in Australia, so the land became covered in dung and parasitic bush flies were everywhere. It wasn't until almost 200 hundred years later that dung beetles were imported to clean up the mess.

Kangaroos are native to Australia and live wild in most parts of the country, growing up to 6 feet tall. They are marsupials, which means the female has a small pouch on her belly where a young kangaroo, called a joey, lives for the first six months. Kangaroos are the national animal of Australia and appear on its coat of arms.

A telegraph is a way of sending a message through a cable, using pulses of electricity. Before telephones and the internet, it was the fastest way of sending a message over a long distance.

Water towers drew water up from the Great Artesian Basin. They were built to fill up the tanks of steam engines.

Up to two million termites live in one termite mound, which can be more than 16 feet tall.

The train would haul a flat-bed truck with tools and extra sleepers so that the crew and passengers could repair the line as they went. Delays were common—the train was once three months late.

The original railroad had to deal with intense heat, flash floods, and the track's wooden sleepers being chewed away by termites. The route followed the telegraph line from Adelaide to Alice Springs, which let Australia communicate with the rest of the world. When termites began to chew through the poles, they were replaced with metal ones, shipped all the way from England.

GREAT ARTESIAN BASIN

The Great Artesian Basin is an enormous body of water trapped in rocks deep beneath Australia. It's more than three times the size of France and 2 miles deep in some places. It is a vital water supply to inland Australia.

The Himalayan mountains are known as the "home of the lightning bolt."

HIMALAYAS

SNOW LEOPARD

MOUNT KANCHENJUNGA

At 28,169 feet tall, Mount Kanchenjunga is the third highest mountain in the world.

DARJEELING

THE TEA TRAIN

KOLKATA TO DARJEELING

from crowded Kolkata, India's sturdy railroads stretch north, escaping the sticky summer heat of the Bengal plains. Trains climb to the cool and misty peaks of the Himalayan mountains, reaching the famous tea fields of Darjeeling.

DARJEELING HILL RAILROAD

Called the "toy train" because of its size, travelers change at New Jalpaiguri for the narrow mountain railroad to Darjeeling.

Elephants wandering onto railroad tracks can be a big problem in West Bengal. Elephants are scared of bees, so speakers near the tracks play the sound of buzzing honey bees to deter them.

NEW JALPAIGURI

At the base of the Himalayas, the busy junction of New Jalpaiguri has rail links to almost all of India, including the capital, New Delhi.

Bengal tigers are the national animal of India, but they are threatened by poaching and loss of habitat.

SOFTSHELL TURTLES

MAIDA

The River Ganges is sacred in Hinduism.

Night-flowering Jasmine is the state flower of West Bengal.

MUGGER CROCODILES

RIVER DOLPHINS

Kolkata's Great Banyan Tree is over 250 years old and one of the world's widest trees. Its circumference is more than 1,083 feet!

KOLKATA

Durga Puja is a huge festival celebrating Durga, the Hindu goddess of war, protection, and strength. Lasting 10 days, it includes feasts, performances, and family visits, ending with processions taking clay idols of Durga into the Ganges River.

GANGES RIVER

RAMPURHAT

BARDDHAMAN

Indian railroads were built by the British Empire, but not for the good of India. The Empire used railroads to make itself richer and more powerful by exporting Indian goods and transporting troops. Now independent, India has a flourishing railroad system of its own that transports passengers around the country cheaply and safely.

Howrah railroad station in Kolkata is India's biggest and busiest.

KOLKATA

The cultural capital of India, Kolkata is known as "the city of joy" and is famous for its vibrant artistic energy. For centuries it was a cornerstone of the British Empire, who extracted valuable tea, spices, and fabrics via its harbor—goods that are a pillar of India's modern economy.

College Street (Boi Para) is more than half a mile long and full of second-hand bookstores.

Kolkata has the only trolley system in South Asia.

Kolkata is the only Indian city with hand-pulled rickshaws.

Cows often wander freely in India because they are sacred to Hindus.

TOY TRAIN STATS:
Distance: 55 miles
Track width: 24 inches
Time: 7 hours 20 minutes
Distance climbed: 2,100 m

The line uses loops and zig-zags to help trains climb the steep hills.

The railroad is a useful tool in the hills and is used as a walkway.

Sand is thrown on the tracks to help the wheels grip the rails on steep slopes.

Since part of the track runs along the road, the train can get stuck in traffic jams.

Townspeople collect hot water from the engine's boiler for their baths.

THE TRAIN

Traveling around tight corners and curves, the "Toy Train" climbs to 7,283 feet above sea level to Darjeeling. Famous for its tea, Darjeeling is known as "the champagne of teas."

A TRIP TO THE
ROOF OF THE WORLD

TEA

Tea is grown in fields and the leaves are picked by hand. They are dried out in the sun, cooked, and rolled to strengthen their flavor.

India grows more than a million tons of tea every year.

Darjeeling tea cannot be grown anywhere else in the world. It is black, with a floral taste, usually drunk without milk.

The East India Company wanted to grow its own tea without depending on China. They started to grow tea in India after botanist Robert Fortune posed as a great nobleman and smuggled leaf samples and tea-making processes out of China. The Chinese plants flourished in the Darjeeling soil.

DARJEELING

The East India Company took control of Darjeeling in 1835. It became a hill station—a place for wealthy British people to escape the summer heat of Calcutta (now called Kolkata). As the Company began to produce tea here, the area became a thriving town. Today, it's a busy city, popular with tourists.

EAST INDIA COMPANY

The East India Company was a tool of the British empire. It took control of land around the world, mining, farming, and trading between its colonies for profit and to strengthen British rule. It was a powerful force in India for centuries. Tea from India became popular in England and helped make the East India Company very rich.

CANFRANC INTERNATIONAL RAILWAY STATION

The "Titanic of the Mountains," this gigantic station was built to be a thriving portal in the Pyrenees Mountains, between France and Spain, but it never quite reached its potential. Witness to fires, Nazi espionage, blocked tunnels, Jewish refugees, and stolen Swiss gold, the station was abandoned in 1970. Today, there are plans to turn the station into a hotel.

ABANDONED STATIONS

The world's railroads are littered with forgotten places which are no longer in use. These "ghost" stations are filled with memories: ticket halls that were once busy with passengers and trains would continuously stop and go.

KYŪ-SHIRATAKI STATION

This station in rural Japan was kept open for years so one high schooler could travel to school. When she graduated, the station closed. Many remote lines in Japan are closing as more families move to big cities.

ALDWYCH TUBE STATION

This London Underground station stored priceless artifacts from the British Museum while the city was bombed in World War II. The end of a branch line which was never finished, it closed in 1994 and is now often used as a film set.

THE RAILWAY OF BONES

Thousands of Russian prisoners died building this unfinished railway through the freezing Arctic tundra. Abandoned in 1953, it may one day be rebuilt, as climate change thaws the frozen ground and makes northern Russia more accessible.

BEGUNKADOR STATION

Passengers and staff deserted this Indian station when rumors spread it was haunted. A traveler claimed to have seen the ghost of a woman in a white sari—and died days later. After closing for 40 years, the station has reopened, but it is still avoided after dark.

HELENSBURGH RAILWAY STATION

Hikers love this abandoned station in the leafy mountains of New South Wales, Australia. The nearby mines it once served have long been closed, and the platforms have been reclaimed by vegetation. Its tunnels shimmer with glow worms, and the ghost of a miner struck by a train is said to haunt the platforms.

CITY HALL SUBWAY STATION

New York's first subway station was abandoned as bigger stations sprouted around it. Well preserved, it's still used as a turnaround for some trains today.

A CITY DIVIDED

Berlin, Germany was divided into two cities in the 20th Century, separated by a wall nobody could cross. But underground trains on lines in the west passed through some stations in the eastern zone. These closed platforms were patrolled by armed guards and nobody was allowed to get off.

PARANAPIACABA STATION

Peering through the mountain mist of southeastern Brazil, a broken clocktower overlooks rotting diesel engines and rusting tracks. It marks the end of a steep mountain railroad built by the British to extract coffee from the Brazilian jungle.

THE REJUVENATION EXPRESS

BEIJING TO HONG KONG

Booming China is famous for great feats of engineering, such as the Great Wall and the Grand Canal. Today, it boasts the longest high-speed railroad in the world, linking the north and south of this vast country in a matter of hours. Rice fields and misty mountains flash past the window in a blur, as the Rejuvenation Express takes passengers between the cranes, factories, and towers of some of the fastest-growing cities on the planet.

BEIJING

China's enormous capital is one of the oldest cities in the world. At its heart is the Forbidden City, a beautiful palace and gardens that were home to the Emperors who ruled China for centuries.

THE REJUVENATION STATS:
Distance: 1,489 miles
Time: 8 hours 58 mins
Top speed: 217 mph
First journey: 2018

With top speeds of 217 mph, the bullet train from Wuhan to Guangzhou is one of the fastest in the world.

The Great Wall of China is the world's biggest manmade structure and took 2,000 years to build.

Stretched end-to-end, the Great Wall could wrap twice around the Moon.

The Shaolin Temple is believed by many to be the birthplace of Chinese martial arts, or Kung-Fu.

GRAND CANAL

YELLOW RIVER

BEIJING

SHIJIAZHUANG

ZHENGZHOU

GRAND CANAL

YELLOW RIVER

YELLOW RIVER

SHAOLIN TEMPLE

SHANGHAI

In Southern China, it is common for people to eat an extra late-night meal after dinner, called Siu Yeh (Ye Xiao). Restaurants and cafes have special Siu Yeh menus, which includes everything from sizzling barbecue pork to creamy custard buns.

YANGTZE RIVER

HONG KONG

Famous for its thriving street food culture, Hong Kong has more restaurants per person than anywhere else in the world. The horizon is packed tight with skyscrapers of the world's biggest banks and businesses, and ferries criss-cross between more than 250 islands, most of which are uninhabited.

Known as "The Chicago of China," Wuhan is famous for Guo Zao, which means, "to have breakfast!" Dishes include Dòu-Pí (fried layers of bean curd and meat) and Rè Gàn Miàn (hot noodles with sesame paste).

Bamboo is used as scaffolding in Hong Kong, because it's lighter and stronger than steel.

GUANGZHOU

SHENZHEN

HONG KONG

The Yangtze River is the longest river in Asia, flowing 3,915 miles.

THREE GORGES DAM

WUHAN

CHANGSHA

Cooked fish heads are a Changsha specialty.

The world's largest power plant generates renewable energy from the power of the Yangtze River. Ships pass through it using a giant elevator.

YANGTZE RIVER

One-third of the world's rice comes from China.

Guangzhou's enormous port was a vital trading center for the Maritime Silk Road more than 2,000 years ago. The route allowed silk, tea, jewels, and porcelain to be traded from China to Europe, via ports including Kolkata and Venice.

China's ancient calendar follows the phases of the Moon. The New Year usually begins in late January or early February and marks the end of winter and the beginning of spring.

Rat

Ox

Tiger

Rabbit

Dragon

Snake

Horse

Goat

Monkey

Rooster

Dog

Pig

CHINESE NEW YEAR

CHINA'S RAILROAD BOOM

Since its first high-speed line in 2008, China has completed more than than 22,000 miles of high-speed tracks—more than the rest of the world combined. The country plans to double this number, linking its cities and towns with some of the fastest trains on the planet.

Red symbolizes joy and good fortune in China.

Hong Kong to Beijing is nine hours by train...

In China, dragons represent Chinese culture, strength, and good luck.

Chinese New Year brings the world's busiest season of travel. Almost all of China follows tradition, returning home and celebrating the Spring Festival with family. Three billion journeys are made during the festivities!

Families celebrate Chinese New Year by eating dumplings and exchanging red envelopes of money.

Fireworks are a Chinese invention.

Chinese writing is a system of symbols, called characters. It is the oldest writing system in use today. 火車站 means "train station." "Train" is made up of the characters for "Fire" (火) and "vehicle" (車).

and 24 hours by car!

BEIJING RAILWAY STATION

To encourage recycling, you can pay for Beijing metro tickets with empty plastic bottles.

TICKETS

THE KINGDOM OF BICYCLES

Half of the world's bikes are made in China, "the kingdom of bicycles." In the 1980s, two-thirds of Beijing's road traffic was bicycles. Cars are more popular today, but there are still half a billion bikes here.

China makes and uses more cars than any other country, which causes heavy traffic and pollution. One Beijing traffic jam lasted nine days! Today, Beijing limits the number of cars on the road—you have to win a lottery to get a license.

ENGLAND

GERMANY

PARIS ★

Cycling is beloved in France—every July the Tour de France finishes in Paris.

CHAMPAGNE REGION

France is well known for its fine food.

Mountainous Switzerland is famous for chocolatiers, cheesemongers, and expert watch and clockmakers. The country stays neutral in all wars, although every 18-year-old Swiss man must join the military for at least six months.

Bees thrive in foresty Slovenia and 1 in 20 people keep bees.

DIJON

THE SIMPLON ORIENT EXPRESS STATS:
Distance: 1,980 miles
Time: 80 hours
Time in operation: 1919-1962

LAKE GENEVA

MONT BLANC

THE ALPS

SWITZERLAND

AUSTRIA

SLOVENIA

SIMPLON TUNNEL

LJUBLJANA

MILAN

ZAGREB

FRANCE

A powerhouse of Italian fashion and finance, glamorous Milan is one of Europe's biggest rail hubs.

VENICE

Venice is sinking by about 1mm every year.

CROATIA

ITALY

THE ALPS

The highest mountain range in Europe spans eight countries. Travelers once took weeks to walk on foot through treacherous passes, resting at "hospices" run by the church. Now trains and highways make it easy— 120 million tourists a year come to visit, hike, and ski.

Italy is internationally known for its rich culture of food, art, and fashion.

With canals and boats instead of roads and cars, the "floating city" of Venice was once a center of global trade, especially of silk, grain, and spice. Today, it draws millions of tourists every year. Despite damage and pollution caused by overcrowding, Venice is often called the most beautiful city in the world.

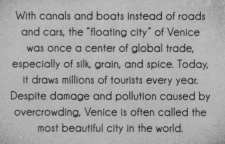

54

THE SIMPLON
ORIENT EXPRESS
PARIS TO ISTANBUL

The most famous train in the world once traveled from the glittering lights of Paris, France, to the mosques and bazaars of Istanbul, Turkey. Forever linked with luxury and intrigue, the route weaved a fine thread through snowy Alpine peaks and sparkling Adriatic shores. The Express survived two wars and heralded the flood of modern tourism that dominates Europe today.

THE DANUBE

World War I began when Austria-Hungary declared war on Serbia.

SERBIA

No stranger to war, Belgrade in Serbia has been battled, besieged, and burned down more than 100 times because of its important position on the Danube and Sava rivers.

ISTANBUL

Europe's largest city, Istanbul, is home to 15 million people and straddles two continents—Europe and Asia. A fusion of Christian and Islamic culture, it has always been a portal between East and West. The city is a vital center for trade: its Grand Bazaar, which first opened in the 15th Century, has more than 7,000 shops and stalls, as well as its own mosque and police station.

BELGRADE
The republic of Yugoslavia was formed after the First World War. It splintered into several nations in the 1990s, including Croatia, Slovenia, and Serbia. They are now popular tourist destinations.

THE DANUBE

THE BALKANS

BLACK SEA

In Bulgaria, shaking your head means "yes," not "no."

ISTANBUL

SOFIA

BULGARIA

TURKEY

Hot mineral springs in Bulgaria's capital, Sofia, have drawn settlers for thousands of years. They remain a tourist attraction today.

Over the decades, several trains called the Orient Express traveled various routes through Europe. The first went via Vienna, with a ferry taking passengers the final leg to Istanbul. This modern-day map shows the route of the "Simplon Orient Express," named for the Simplon Tunnel, which took the train beneath the Alps.

THE MEDITERRANEAN

The crowded Bosporus strait connects the Black Sea to the Mediterranean. Strategically vital for thousands of years, today it's used by tankers shipping oil from Russia to Europe and the United States.

GREECE

The Orient Express was the brainchild of George Nagelmackers, inventor of the European sleeping carriage, or Wagon-Lit. He dreamed of a Europe open to discovery, and hoped his trains would link the continent together. Shuttling Europe's rich and famous across borders in comfort and style, the luxurious train quickly became a hotbed of intrigue, espionage, excess, and adventure.

The many Orient Express routes survived the shifting powers of two World Wars, but the service was suspended until peace was declared.

SIMPLON TUNNEL

This 12-mile rail tunnel beneath the Alps was once the longest in the world, unlocking fast rail links to Southern Europe. Nazis tried to blow it up in 1945, but were thwarted by Italian resistance.

The Armistice ending World War I was signed in an Orient Express dining car. Hitler later seized the carriage in World War II and had it destroyed.

Crossing the borders of so many countries, the Express was notorious for transporting secret agents.

THE SPIES' EXPRESS

Many royals rode the train. The King of Bulgaria insisted on driving it, which he did at hair-raising speed.

An American naval attaché with a briefcase of secret papers was pushed out of the train.

HIDDEN IN THE MOUNTAINS

Much of the Swiss transport network is rumored to be rigged to explode. Railroad bridges, road tunnels, and mountain passes can supposedly be detonated to protect the country from invasion. There is also secret bunkers, tunnels, and artillery hidden in the Alps.

MURDER ON THE ORIENT EXPRESS

Agatha Christie, the world's greatest detective novelist, often rode the train to the Middle East with her archaeologist husband. Inspired by a real murder on board when the train was caught in a snowdrift, she penned the bestselling *Murder on the Orient Express*.

Many suspicious deaths took place on board. A wealthy woman was robbed of her jewels and furs and thrown from her compartment window.

The Orient Express was the first train to serve ice.

The train's glamour began to fade in the 50s and 60s as the rich began to fly by luxury jet. The Simplon Orient Express was replaced by a slower train in 1962. Today, a luxury replica travels the route to Venice.

JASPER NATIONAL PARK

The line travels through the largest nature reserve in the Canadian Rockies. Along the route, thick forests bristle with wildlife and lakes glisten in the shadow of tall, snow-capped mountains.

CANADA

Canada built the world's first UFO landing pad to welcome any aliens that might visit.

VANCOUVER

With the North Shore Mountains as its backdrop, picturesque Vancouver ballooned from a small town into a metropolis with the arrival of the transcontinental railroad in 1887. Today, relaxed Vancouver is considered one of the world's best places to live.

EDMONTON

SAINT PAUL ALBERTA

JASPER

SASKATOON

Sprawling Edmonton boasts the largest shopping mall in North America. It is home to the world's tallest indoor rollercoaster.

Highways through Canada's national parks have bridges and tunnels designed for wildlife to safely cross the road.

When digging a well for water, the railroad builders found natural gas instead. They used the gas to heat their stations.

VANCOUVER

THE
CANADIAN

VANCOUVER TO TORONTO

Eighty five percent of the world's maple syrup comes from Canada.

A mammoth journey of more than 2,700 miles, The Canadian connects the distant cities of Toronto and Vancouver, linking the east and the west coast of the world's second largest country. Crossing vast wetlands, open prairies, and the misty forests of the Rocky Mountains, the journey bristles with wildlife beneath a wide open sky.

The Canadian Shield is an enormous, visible part of Earth's crust. It's thinner in Northern Ontario, meaning gravity is slightly weaker there—people weigh less here than elsewhere on Earth.

CANADIAN SHIELD

Canada's national dish is poutine—fries with cheese curds and gravy on top.

The Narcisse Snake Dens are home to tens of thousands of red-sided garter snakes.

NARCISSE SNAKE DENS

The train drops off passengers at "flag stops" only by request. Many are only accessible by train... or canoe!

TORONTO

Once called York by British settlers in the 18th Century, Toronto is Canada's largest city. It is known for its sports and music scene. One fifth of all Canadians live in the area around it, called the Golden Horseshoe.

WINNIPEG

The Canadian Pacific Railway company was founded in 1881 to link Canada's coasts by rail, becoming one of the biggest transport systems in the world.

Twenty percent of the world's fresh water is in Canada

LAKE SUPERIOR

SUDBURY JUNCTION

Winnipeg is covered in snow for about 130 days a year. In winter, the city has the world's longest skating rink—a frozen river over 5 miles long.

LAKE HURON

TORONTO

LAKE MICHIGAN

NIAGARA FALLS

THE CANADIAN STATS:
Distance: 2,763 miles
Time: 4 days
First journey: 1955

CHICAGO

NEW YORK

UNITED STATES OF AMERICA

When a bald eagle loses a feather, it will shed another on the opposite wing to keep itself perfectly balanced.

European settlers hunted bison almost to extinction, and many First Nations families starved.

JOURNEY THROUGH CANADA

The First Nations are Indigenous societies who lived in Canada before the arrival of European settlers. There are more than 600 distinct First Nation governments in Canada today. For some, the introduction of the railroad to Canada in the 19th Century was a symbol of progress and wealth. But for First Nations and other Indigenous peoples, the railroad is a symbol of how they lost their land to a continuing influx of European settlers.

Some rare Canadian black bears are born with white fur. First Nations consider them sacred and call them "spirit bears."

Thousands of Indigenous people died from diseases, such smallpox and influenza, brought to Canada by European settlers.

Many Indigenous peoples make decisions using the Seventh Generation Principle: how will decisions made today affect the next seven generations.

Coyotes are important in First Nation folktales. They often appear as a crafty trickster and are sometimes involved in the creation of the land itself.

Moose can swim, diving 20 feet to eat underwater plants.

More than 522,000 miles of oil pipelines criss-cross Canada, pumping millions of barrels of oil a week. Drilling for oil can harm the environment and poison drinking water.

Royal Canadian Mounted Police, or "Mounties," are Canada's national police force. They are famous for their wide hats and red uniforms.

Canada moves most of its farm produce by rail. One car of grain can be worth $23,000.

"Sanders" are tubes on a locomotive that blast sand towards a train's wheels. This helps to provide grip in icy or wet weather.

Canoes and kayaks were invented by people of the First Nations. They originally crafted them using tree trunks and animal skins. First Nations peoples also invented darts, cough syrup, and lacrosse—one of Canada's national sports.

Recently, many Indigenous groups have united against oil pipelines being built through their land. The First Nations-led protests block trains passing through their reservations. Train blockades can paralyze Canada's businesses.

Beavers are nature's engineers. Their giant orange teeth cut down trees, which they use to build dams and canals helping to reduce flooding. Canada once had beavers the size of bears! Beavers' fur was considered very valuable and the fur trade drew many European settlers to Canada.

OTHER EPIC JOURNEYS

The world is full of amazing railroad adventures!

Here are some more to discover.

THE REUNIFICATION EXPRESS

The steel backbone of Vietnam's railroads links the north to the south. After being damaged in a long civil war, the repaired railroad is a symbol of a united Vietnam.

Busy trains rattle through crowded Hanoi, inches from houses.

VIETNAM

★ HANOI

PERFUME RIVER
Flowers from orchards upstream fall into the river in fall, making the water smell like perfume.

HAI VAN ("OCEAN CLOUD") PASS

The Ocean Cloud Pass is named for the mists that rise from the sea. Steep and rocky, it's as dangerous as it is beautiful.

HO CHI MINH CITY
In bustling Ho Chi Minh, there are 20 motorcycles for every car.

HO CHI MINH CITY

THE EGYPTIAN SLEEPER

Tracing Egypt from head to toe, this overnight adventure clanks over the same sands trodden by Pharaohs. From glittering skyscrapers to snapping crocodiles, it's the perfect way to explore 4,000 years of Egyptian civilization.

ALEXANDRIA

NILE DELTA

Trains in Egypt carried cotton to markets in the Nile Delta.

CAIRO

Once the world's largest city, Alexandria was home to the Great Library, the most significant seat of knowledge in the ancient world. Through fire and war, the library and its contents were lost forever.

Egypt's thriving capital is home to the Great Pyramids, built more than 4,500 years ago as tombs for Pharaohs. They were made by hand from two million blocks of stone.

EGYPT

THE NILE

LUXOR

They city of Luxor lies within Thebes, one of the world's oldest inhabited cities. Among its many ancient monuments are the Karnak temples, said to be where the god Amun-Ra, creator of the universe, lived on Earth.

The Aswan Dam generates hydroelectricity and controls the flow of the Nile River, preventing floods and droughts.

ASWAN

THE TRANS-PYRENEAN EXPRESS

From the mouth-watering meals of Lyon to the bustling beaches of Barcelona, the high-speed French TGV makes an effortless dash through the towering Pyrenees, linking two of Europe's most celebrated cities in a matter of hours.

The Pyrenees mountains link the Atlantic Ocean and Mediterranean Sea, separating France and Spain. They're home to "Le Petit Train Jaune," the little yellow train, which climbs to Bolquère-Eyne, the highest station in France.

FRANCE

Andorra is a tiny country nestled between France and Spain. It is less than a third of the size of London.

Llívia is a Spanish town surrounded by France. This is called an enclave—where part of one country is surrounded by another.

LYON

Lyon's streets are undercut by secretive Traboules—passageways once used by French Resistance fighters to escape the Nazis in WWII. The city is also home to the Lumiere brothers, the inventors of movies.

LLÍVIA

SPAIN   **THE PYRENEES**

ANDORRA

Sunkissed Barcelona is famous for beautiful buildings like the Sagrada Familia, a cathedral that has taken more than 200 years to build so far—longer than the Pyramids.

Flamingos gather each year on the Camargue salt marshes in the south of France. Their gray feathers turn pink from eating algae and invertebrates. A group of flamingos is called a "flamboyance."

BARCELONA

THE COPPER CANYON RAILWAY

Rising from the thriving port of Los Mochis to the inland city of Chihuahua, this railroad crosses six treacherous "copper canyons" named for their red and green walls. Taking 90 years to finish, this is one of Mexico's only passenger trains.

STEEP CLIMB
The train snakes expertly to great heights: one tunnel conceals a 180-degree-turn while the train climbs 98 feet. Four times as big as the Grand Canyon and about one mile deep, these canyons were carved out by ancient rivers.

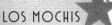

OJINAGA

CHIHUAHUA
This city was made famous by the dogs. The chihuahua is the world's smallest dog breed.

EL DIVISADERO

A 1.- mile zip line across the canyon at El Divisadero sends you flying at speeds of up to 81 mph..

COPPER CANYON

LOS MOCHIS

Copper Canyon is famous for silver. Mexico is the world's largest producer of silver.

MEXICO

The indigenous Tarahumara people are renowned for being the world's best runners. Some are known to have run 124 miles at a time.

THE NEXT STOP

Hopefully you've enjoyed traveling the world by rail and discovered parts of the globe you never knew about before.

Railroads are great vehicles to connect us, but it is important not to forget full stories of how these railroads came to be. Many of the world's railroads were first built to exploit, oppress, or steal from people. This caused great harm to so many and must not be forgotten.

However, we can still appreciate the spectacular feats of ingenuity that remain part of our railroads today. Trains can help us discover and better understand the world. So always travel with a good heart and an open mind.

Trains were at the forefront of the Industrial Revolution, which reshaped our world forever. They were once cutting-edge technology. But as planes and cars became cheaper and more conevnient, passengers abandoned the comfort of long-distance trains.

But today, trains are becoming more popular. Climate change has made us feel conflicted about traveling by polluting cars and planes, and many modern passenger trains are powered by electricity, producing little or no emissions at all as they travel along.

Instead of standing in line for hours at airports, more travelers are choosing an easy ride on comfortable trains, passing beautiful scenery, and linking the heart of one city directly to another. New railroad lines are being built all over the world, opening up exciting new routes to discover. As more people realize the joy and environmental benefits of traveling by train, railroads will remain part of our lives for good.

Bon voyage!

About the author
Sam Sedgman is an award-winning author of the bestselling Adventures on Trains series. He lives in London, U.K, and travels whenever he can. He grew up with a railroad line at the bottom of his backyard and has loved trains ever since.

About the illustrator
Sam Brewster is a freelance illustrator and filmmaker. He's partial to all kinds of trains—especially rollercoasters, miniature railroads, funiculars, and monorails!